VVI IL I\

CANCER CALLS,

ANSWER

A Story of Acceptance,
Resilience, and Self-Love

WHEN
CANCER CALLS,
ANSWER

A Story of Acceptance, Resilience, and Self-Love

VERO LEMAY

Vero Lemay, 1975 -
https://verolemay.com

ISBN 978-1-9991046-0-3 (Paperback)
ISBN 978-1-9991046-1-0 (eBook)

Edited by Melissa McLeod
Book Cover design by Franny Armstrong
Book production by Dawn James, Publish and Promote
Perseus Design, Ebook & Interior Layout & Design,
Photographer, Vince Amato

The information in this book is not intended as a substitute for medical or professional advice or treatment. It is strictly the opinion of the author. It is recommended that you consult your professional healthcare provider if you have any physical, mental, or emotional health concerns. In the event you use any of this information in this book for yourself, the author and the publisher assume no responsibility for your actions.

Printed and bound in Canada

DEDICATION

This book is dedicated to my mother and father without who this book would not be possible. I also want to acknowledge the loves of my life: Sylvain, Alys and Lily-Rose, and finally my Starfish Tribe.

CONTENTS

INTRODUCTION

How this book came to be: I felt compelled to write the one book that I desperately needed to read when I was diagnosed again with cancer, this time it was stage 4 and incurable. I thought about writing a book that would walk you through my healing journey slowly and gently, as a mother would hold her child's hand while strolling through tall grass. Then, I listened to my inner author who insisted, *you need to inspire them to make a change. You must make them show up in their lives!*

Forgive my enthusiastic and assertive tone, I am writing this book from a place of urgency to convince you that you have it in you. You are everything and you have everything you need to heal! Now let's roll up our sleeves and start this exciting journey to your new life where YOU are in control. Time to answer, because cancer's calling!

"If you don't make time for your wellness, you will be forced to make time for your illness."

-Anonymous

CHAPTER 1

THOSE THREE WORDS

July 6, 2017, the day before my 42nd birthday, I visited my oncologist's office. My husband and I were trying to make small talk as we waited. The room was packed with cancer patients and their caregivers. We decided to stand. I didn't mind standing. I did not want to sit amongst them. I did not want to be part of that community once more. I remember trying to entertain my husband by laughing at his awkward jokes. Yet, I kept thinking that the moments to come would alter my life and those whom I love. I imagined my daughters, my parents, my brother, and my friends. Every single one of them had told me not to worry, that this appointment was just a precautionary measure. All, but one, my sister-in-law and dear friend, Fannie, had another outlook. I had shared with her my concerns about the cancer being back; that the x-rays showed spots on my lungs, and that the oncologist scheduled an appointment to share results. Contrary to my brother Ben, who kept saying not to worry that it was nothing, she said, "You know what? You're right. The cancer is probably back. But you are not alone. We did this once, we will do it again!" She, I thought, would be able to handle the news. In retrospect, the way Fannie responded to my insecurities was probably the best way anyone could. She reminded me that no matter how bad life gets, we are not alone.

As the morning minutes passed slowly—10:43, 10:44 …, I felt scared out of my mind. My husband would smile, hug me, and try to make me laugh. Finally, after what seemed to be endless hours of mental agony, the oncologist invited us in. In that small, white, cold room, I heard the words I never wanted to hear again in my life. "You have cancer." If you have ever heard those three words strung together, you know exactly what those words do to you, to your family, to your entire world. One can only hope to never hear those words, but for me, this was the second time and just a few days short of being medically considered in remission. This time, the words "You have cancer" came with a bonus: it travelled to my lungs, evolved to a stage 4, incurable cancer. No one can prepare you to hear those three words but now...*incurable*? A wave of hopelessness came over me as I looked at my husband who wilted over with sadness. I kept thinking: *Why me? Why again? How can life be so unfair?* Then with a heavy lump in my throat, I courageously uttered, "What can you do?" My oncologist looked me straight in the eyes. She was young, efficient, and cared for me for the past five years. I trusted her with my life. The look on her face was one I had never seen. It was a look of sadness mixed with pity. Not very reassuring, I took a breath and looked down. She proceeded to explain that I had too many metastases for radiotherapy. She would be puncturing my lungs with numerous small holes making it impossible for me to breathe. As for chemotherapy, she continued, it was effective for fast, aggressive cancers, something my cancer was not. Her hands were tied. There was nothing she or any other medical practitioner could do. I swallowed hard and squeezed my husband's hand. It took all the strength I had left not to be reduced to tears. Choked up, I softly asked, "What can I do?" In the gentlest tone possible, she responded "Nothing. Enjoy life." What? Enjoy life? How can I enjoy life now? What life? I am incurable? I will die. I melted in my chair in hopes of disappearing, forever.

Unfortunately, "We will monitor the evolution," and, "Good luck, Mrs. Lemay," were the only other sentences that were spoken to me that day in the hospital. That is until my husband managed to whimper out a few words as we took what felt like an eternity to walk back to the car.

"I don't want you to die. I can't do this without you." I remember feeling numb from head to toe. Every part of my body shook. I was shivering, freezing, as the warm sun shone on us. I looked at him and said, "I can't do this right now. I can't be there to help you with this. I have cancer."

By then, I was sobbing uncontrollably and so was he. We finally made it to our car both silent and broken. He tried to hold back his tears as he was driving but I could see his cheeks were soaking wet as the tears continuously rolled down his eyes.

Oh, hell no! Here we go again. I stared blankly out the window. Silence.

The hours that followed were some of the most painful in my life. We have two beautiful daughters, Lily-Rose, 13, and Alys, 16 at the time. How do you tell someone you love that you have cancer? Having done it twice, let me assure you there is no easy or right way to do this, and it certainly does not get easier with practice. With the little energy we had left, we called the girls to join us on the couch. Alys was accompanied by her boyfriend Charles at the time, and I remember thinking, good, at least she will have extra moral support. Alys was strong. She had undergone a kidney transplant a few years back and knew how very precious life is. She was also wise beyond years yet reacted violently to my first cancer diagnosis, very out of character for her. How would she react to this terrible news now? Lily-Rose followed up the stairs and was just staring at me blankly. She could see we were upset. She sat all curled up at the very end of the sofa. Lily-Rose learned very early on that the people she loved could die young. Watching her sister go through kidney failure, dialysis, and ending up with a kidney transplant changed her "happy-go-lucky" attitude. She was only eight when she learned to fake a smile and be a pillar for the family as I faced cancer. She was much too little to have been disillusioned like that. All three of their precious young faces showed fear and sadness. Sitting between the girls, Charles held both their hands firmly as if to say, "I got you." I shuffled over to the coffee table and sat down on it alongside my husband. I could feel my heart beating in my throat. I knew that with my next words I was going to turn their world upside down. My poor babies had already lost so much of their childhood worrying about death. And I was going to do this to them again. I didn't even finish my sentence which went something like, "My loves, I did not get the best news today…" before both my daughters cried out a shrieking, "Nooo!" The news was too much to bear for the family. Tears, screams, swearing, and the look in their eyes. That look of pity mixed with desperation. It's a look you don't ever want to see in your loved one's eyes. I am their mother. I am supposed to be their rock and protector, the invincible source of strength and love. How can I do this to them again? So much anger and guilt rumbled in my body but I was paralyzed with fear. All I could feel was defeat. I thought: *Cancer, you have taken everything from me.*

The next several weeks were a blur. Days turned to nights, nights turned to days. To put it simply, I was emotionally and physically unavailable. I couldn't even fake a smile when my daughters came home from school, let alone have the energy to get up and cook a meal. I was alone in my head. My inner voice kept saying, *"This is your fault, Véro. You brought this on."* Not the most supporting actress my inner voice, you might be thinking, but you know what? She was right.

Now, I am not saying that I wanted cancer to return and that I purposely sabotaged my health. However, the level of stress I was under and the lifestyle choices I made were not ideal, to say the least. I had just finished one of the most emotionally draining school years, teaching 23 first-grade students. I remember closing my classroom door at the end of everyday thinking; Wow! These poor little ones have so much to deal with. I had students living through abuse, neglect, severe learning difficulties, and poverty; students who went home every night to adults that could not love them or take care of their needs. I would go to bed with the thought of my student's suffering and wake up with the same thoughts haunting me. They are only children! Why is life so unfair? I remember joking with my colleague, Veronik, a devoted special needs attendant, saying I should put a sign above my classroom door that reads: Home of the Lost Souls. My classroom was a meeting point for numerous children that were not even my students. They came at lunchtime, during recess, or when they were kicked out of class. They came to get hugs, mostly, and to talk. My classroom became a haven for many. I was just a teacher, not a psychologist. Still, I did my best and gave them a soft place to land. But at what price?

My job took a lot out of me and I found myself emotionally drained by the time 2:30 pm came. No time to rest though, my second work shift had already started. My daughters and my eldest's boyfriend were lined up at my classroom door ready to go home. They too had their issues and conflicts that needed my attention. I had to show up and be a mom to them. I would not be less patient or less caring. They were my precious daughters and I did all I could to give them the love, attention, and devotion they deserved, regardless of how difficult my day was. Now don't get me wrong, I am by no means a perfect parent, I know my girls have many stories about me having, "a squirrel brain", or "losing it", but I guess we will save those stories for another book.

As for my health habits, I led an average active lifestyle and considered myself mostly healthy. I would go for walks a few times a week. I prepared healthy meals (so I thought) most of the week but treated myself to fast foods as well. I also loved Jelly Belly Candies. I even had a jar filled with them that was labelled, "Chill Pills". A little sugar never hurt anyone, right?

I was conscious that the behaviours described above probably helped lead to cancer, but how do I change? How do I take proper care of myself? Where do I start? What should I eat?

All these questions were flooding my thoughts. I desperately needed answers, but sadly I came to realize that in my case, those answers were not to be found at the oncologist office. When none of the typical procedures, such as chemotherapy, work for you then you're pretty much abandoned. Left to die. I was drowning here, and all the medical world had to offer was a good luck card, not even "get well" because they knew that wasn't going to happen. Who was going to rescue me? Help!

Thus, I began my lonely journey to understand how this came to be. I began to deepen my understanding of my life patterns that were promoting cancer and weakening my immune system. The mere fact of being diagnosed with cancer causes deep trauma in your body. Add to that a diet that contained processed foods and sugar, along with a stressful job and very little me time. I had set a trap myself and walked right into it.

I have set out on a quest to heal and I encourage you to do the same. Cancer might be calling, but you are not alone. You have this book to guide you. You will take back the power that is too often given solely to your doctor(s). You will get through this and thrive.

*"Not all storms come to disrupt your life;
some come to clear your path."*

-Anonymous

CHAPTER 2

YOU HAVE THE POWER TO HEAL

After a few months filled with anger, depression, and resentment went by, I decided that if the medical world had abandoned me then I would seek out another type of doctor that could provide answers. I didn't feel optimistic, but I owed it to my family to at least try to seek out alternative help. They had seen enough of the helpless woman, mom, and wife sitting on the couch in her pyjamas staring at the wall

all day. I first asked around to see who the best naturopath in the region was and found a highly qualified one nearby.

Walking in her office felt completely different than walking into the oncologist 's office. It was lighter with no one in the waiting room. I felt calmer, almost relaxed. I already had my death sentence. I knew that nothing I would hear that day could be worse. When I was called into her room, I was struck by her beauty and youth. She was pregnant and sat at her desk with a large pillow on her tummy. I later learned she was doing this to protect the baby from the computer's radiation. She was very thorough. She reviewed my medical background and explained that my immune system had been weak for a very long time. She was knowledgeable. She taught me what cancer cells were: unrecognizable mutated cells; what they fed on: sugar; where they prosper better: in an acidic body. She prescribed me a strict Keto diet and many supplements. I walked out of there feeling a little less hopeless and a lot more curious about what was happening in my body!

When I got home that night, my family doctor called me. He is an amazing person who always goes above and beyond for his patients. His voice was meek as he said, "Um, I have no words." I thought that was strange and asked what was the matter? "Well, I just started to watch the documentary series, The Truth About Cancer, and I am rethinking the integrity of my profession," he said. "I am sitting on the kitchen floor, disillusioned. You need to watch this!"

Remember, this was my family doctor, a man of science. He was telling me that the medical world might not know it all. That there may be another way to do this. From that moment on, I decided I was going to be a student. I would learn from everyone all I could about cancer.

I followed my doctor's advice and watched the documentary "The Truth about Cancer"[1]. It was a real eye-opener, to say the least. Ty Bollinger, the creator of this documentary series, had interviewed patients, herbalists, naturopaths, and doctors. They all had one thing in common: they looked at cancer differently. On one hand, I was shocked by the corruption and false advertising offered by the pharmaceutical industry. On the other, I was in awe of all the seemingly ordinary people who healed their cancer with alternative measures.

However, it wasn't until I met another naturopath, Nadège, that I experienced "the shift". When I was initially diagnosed with cancer, the first time around, I saw it as my enemy. It did not belong to me. It was something I had to fight and most of all, survive. I used to say things such as, "the cancer" I have is in my salivary gland, or, "the cancer" is not part of me. Wrong! And here's why: your body created this cancer, so it is entirely yours. Your very own, custom made, cancer. This may be difficult to hear but please keep an open mind and allow me to elaborate further.

Nadège invited me to sit down in her little wooden hut by a warm fire and she began to explain what cancer was. She started by saying that this cancer is *my* cancer. My body created it because it wants me to live. My body had tried in a variety of ways to let me know I was in trouble. I had not listened thus it created the least possible damaging condition for me to listen. For me, the least possible damaging condition was stage 4 cystic adenoid cancer with metastasis in the lungs. I guess cancer had been calling for a while, but my ringer was off! Was I going to answer now and see what it had been trying to tell me for so long?

This naturopath encouraged me to reflect on my lifestyle and choices. As I began reflecting on the questions listed below, I realized that cancer was telling me that I was lacking *self-love*. I hardly had any time for me in my life. I was feeling stressed at work and powerless. The fact that cancer was in my lungs was literally suffocating me, making it more difficult for me to breathe. Nadège explained to me that I was unable to discern what was mine and what belonged to others. I was taking on everyone's problems and living with them. Being a mother, a wife, and a first-grade teacher, you can imagine how many issues dealt with daily. I realized that it was as if had the emergency button activated, permanently flashing red and ringing, but sadly enough, I didn't pay attention. Cancer tried to warn me.

This wise woman was also the first one to speak to me about how powerful our thoughts are. She offered me tea and a blanket and asked, "What is your dream?" I accepted her offerings and answered without hesitation, "To rock my grandkids to sleep." She looked me straight in the eyes and replied, "Wrong!" This left me perplexed. How can this woman, whom I just met, tell me that my dreams are wrong? She continued, "That cannot be your dream and you know why." I stared at her puzzled by her comment, wanting her to feed me the answer to her question, but she did not budge. She offered no extra information. I thought for a few minutes and suddenly I felt a wave of sadness overcome my body. I could not breathe. I broke down in tears: "Because after that I would die!" I sobbed like a baby. She was right! What would happen *after* I became a Grandma? Would I have no purpose and die? My life goal could not be based solely on being a grandma. That could not be my ultimate dream. Nadège also explained that my daughters may never have kids because subconsciously they knew it was the end goal for me. When I was able to stop crying and speak, I shared another dream of mine—to learn all I could about cancer, to heal and help others heal. To this, she smiled and said, "Now, *that* is a good dream."

After that very enlightening meeting, I never saw my cancer, or my body for that matter, in the same light again. I understood that our mind is an extremely powerful tool and that we must use it wisely. I knew my body was my best friend and that cancer was her messenger. I was ready to listen and here is what she said: *Yes, you created this cancer but because you created this, you can heal it.* Now, that is empowering! You have the power to heal yourself. Cancer may have been fabricated due to poor eating habits, lifestyle, stress, unresolved issues, weak immune system, but we have all we need within us to change. Everyone is different so all cancers are different as well. I could no longer live in denial. I needed to act so I started looking at the habits and patterns that might have caused my cancer. Time for self-reflection.

Here are a few questions I asked myself. I recommend you do the same.

1. **Nutrition.** What kinds of food am I feeding myself? Do I choose organic products? What about processed foods? Am I a sugar addict?

2. **Exercise.** What kind of exercise do I engage in (if any)? How often do I exercise? How many times a week?

3. **Environment.** What is my home life like? How is my relationship with my family? What about work?

4. **Mindfulness.** What part of my day is dedicated to relaxation? Do I meditate?

Do I know how to live in the present moment?

5. **Thoughts.** What dreams do I have? What self-talk do I have? Do I believe in myself?

Take the time to answer these questions truthfully. Are you seeing an area where you have neglected your mind, body, and/or soul?

What did I do after some introspection? I went on to further my research with a newfound curiosity. I highly recommend you read *Radical Remissions, Surviving Cancer against All Odds* written by Kelly A. Turner, PH.D.[2] It provides inspiring stories about recovery, remission, and possibilities. Chapter 6, "Increasing Positive Emotions", teaches us that instead of asking questions such as, *Why me?* We should say: *I'm listening. What am I supposed to learn?* Reminding us, to be mindful of our thoughts. The way we perceive what is happening to us directly influences the outcome of what will be. If you have negative self-talk and think about being powerless in the face of cancer, then chances are you will be. However, if you change your inner-dialogue to a more positive one, including messages of empowerment and even conviction that you can heal, then chances are you will do just that. Be mindful of what thoughts enter your head. The body listens to what the mind tells it.

Bad news, you have cancer. Good news, you created it so you can heal it! You have the power to nurture your cancer and *reclaim your health*.

"Sometimes what you are most afraid of doing is the very thing that will set you free."

-Anonymous

CHAPTER 3

READY AND
WILLING TO LISTEN

Sarah, a good friend of mine, uttered the sentence that my intuition needed to hear to manifest herself. "We have Guanabana here, in Costa Rica."

I know that sounds like a pretty trivial string of words, but for me, it was the spark that ignited an internal fire. For several months, I had been on a quest, seeking an alternative way to heal my cancer. Many of my loved ones felt the need to share numerous tips, superfoods, magic pills, new research all in the hopes that this would be the quick fix I needed. My friend Susanna, a cancer thriver, had also experienced this overwhelming amount of advice. She still, however, felt the urge to share something with me. It was a Facebook post about a super fruit called Guanabana. Receiving well-intentioned advice, tips, and miracle cures from friends and family members often becomes part of being a cancer patient and often leaves us with more questions than answers. However, something about Guanabana stuck with me.

Guanabana, also known as soursop, is a tropical fruit that grows in South and Central America. The fruit is extremely sugary but its leaves, when infused and consumed as a tea, become tumour zappers. At the time, the leaves were illegal in Canada, as they were deemed too potent. Imagine, no conventional medicine or research projects were interested in me and my cancer and now, even the natural world was putting up barricades.

When my friend Sarah called and said "We have Guanabana" it was a message of hope. It was like a switch was turned on inside me. At that very moment, I knew I had to go to Costa Rica. I didn't know why exactly and surely didn't know how I'd get there. Let's just say money was becoming an issue in our house. Still, I was perplexed by my need to go there. Sarah offered the opportunity to go visit on several occasions, she said it would boost my morale. However, I was not in the best of spirits, feeling defeated, with little energy, and I knew I wouldn't make good company. But that one sentence was able to put all those concerns to rest. All that "poor me" self-talk went out the window and brought in a conviction that this was where I needed to be.

I can only attribute this pull to Costa Rica as my inner voice calling me. I remember watching Wayne Dyer's documentary, "The Shift[3]" where he explains that there comes a moment in your life where you feel compelled to do something you normally wouldn't. The pull you feel is so strong and most likely out of character. I remember watching this in tears thinking when am I going to get that change to break away and shift my life?

It had been a long tormenting seven months since my recurrence diagnosis, and I guess I was finally ready to act. That evening, when my husband came back from work, I was ready with my sales pitch. He listened to me and told me that my health was also his priority and that we will make it happen. My daughters listened from a distance and agreed that a vacation would do me good. A week later, I was on a plane ready to live what was going to be the most life-changing 10 days of my life.

It was my first time travelling alone yet I had no fears. I didn't feel lonely. After teaching small children for 22 years and raising two of my own, some alone time felt just right—and long overdue! I felt free and empowered. Feelings that had been foreign to me for a long time.

The seats next to me on the plane were empty and I was able to stretch my legs and take a nap. The universe was finally in my favour, I thought. The flight flew by quickly and before I knew it, I landed in the land of promise, Costa Rica.

Once I set foot in a beautiful coastal town called Uvita, I felt guided. I saw signs everywhere. I first opted to try a yoga class. I started practicing yoga back home with a group of elderly people, as I was not up to the challenge of performing a Sun Salutation (a sequence of movements that builds up body heat) in front of my peers. I knew this class was different the moment I walked onto the jungle platform. It was surrounded by nature and the only sounds we heard were the songs of tropical birds. The class was about a lot more than the asanas, the poses. I had to hold in my tears as Pilar, the teacher, who later became a dear friend, spoke about the heart chakra and self-love. I felt as though she was talking to me personally and her words touched my heart. I knew that I had not been in love with myself even though I always thought I loved me.

I recall my first walk on the beach. I could not help but feel guided. The air was hot and humid. It smelled of sea salt and ylang ylang. On this beach, I discovered a beautiful two-coloured heart-shaped rock. On another visit, a black and white dog with a black heart-shaped marking on his side dropped a coconut at my feet to play catch with him. Later, there was a tree in the middle of the jungle with a poster stapled to it that read, "This tree is the tree of love. Hug it and let it heal your broken heart." I felt like everywhere I turned I could see a heart or another symbol of love.

Remember, nothing felt right for the last seven months, except maybe meeting Nadège. It was the first time I started making true connections within me. Once we start to quiet our minds, we can observe the signs that are all around us. I was finally ready to listen. *Go on cancer, what do you want me to know?*

I learned so many lessons in only a few days in that warm tropical country. One day as we were strolling on the beach, Nikki, Sarah's youngest daughter, looked up at me and said, "Véro, you know coconuts are more dangerous than crocodiles?" She meant that in Costa Rica more people get killed by falling coconuts than by crocodile attacks. I laughed at her remark and playful smile. Immediately, I thought, is that not just like cancer? Cancer can hit anyone at any time without any warning, just like a coconut. Yet, we are all too busy looking out for "crocodiles" to even think that coconuts could get us. We are too busy going on with our lives, our work, our stressful obligations, and too busy keeping up with the Joneses.

The most amazing encounter of my healing journey happened in that first short trip to the tropical paradise. I met Aida. Aida is a local herbalist whose knowledge had been passed down from generation to generation. It was my friend Sarah who heard about her one windy afternoon as she was frantically running around her front porch trying to collect Guanabana leaves that were flying left and right. She had hung them to dry, preparing for my arrival, but the wind took hold of them. It was then that her neighbour asked what she was doing? Sarah replied that she was drying these leaves for her friend who had cancer. Her neighbour immediately blurted out, "You have to meet Aida!" Sarah decided to listen to her neighbour and let Guanabana lead the way. After all, this too must be a sign. It was Guanabana that was bringing her friend, she thought. She decided to meet Aida first and let her know about my condition. I think she went ahead without me because she wanted to see if she was the real deal and could help, and to protect me from disappointment if it was not the case. Sarah knew that I was fragile and did not want me to be misguided or disappointed.

Aida was surrounded by nature and had an open kitchen with chickens running in and out of the house as she concocted interesting remedies. The worst part, Sarah tells me, was when Aida explained to her that my treatment would involve a plant cleanse and ingesting snake oil. To this day, Sarah giggles when she speaks about her unique meeting with Aida, "Had I known I would have had to pick your medicine off of trees in the jungle, I wouldn't have worn flip flops!"

When Sarah mentioned the details of her visit with this elderly plant lady, I was not shocked, I wanted to meet this unique woman. Heck, what do I have to lose? Sarah agreed to take me with a smirk on her face and said, "If you say so!"

My first meeting with Aida is to this day one of my most treasured moments, even if it did involve me drinking snake oil. It had taken a good 15 minutes of driving up a winding, dirt road into the jungle to get to her home. When we arrived, she was waiting for us at an outdoor table overlooking the ocean with the most beautiful views. In front of her were piles of leaves, a jar of hot tea, glasses, and yes, you guessed it, a jar of snake oil.

She only spoke Spanish. My Spanish at the time was non-existent, so she called her daughter Jaz for backup. I began to explain to Jaz why I was there and what my condition was all the while sitting across from Aida and sensing her fixation on me. I explained how I had a recurrence of cancer and that it was now in my lungs. Jaz translated and Aida laughed! I thought something was lost in translation, but Jaz explained that Aida laughed because she thought I would say, stage 4 pancreatic cancer and that condition would have been a little more difficult to treat.

Wait, my cancer was simple enough to treat? You can imagine the look on my face at that comment. *What?* Since when do you hear stage 4 incurable cancer and simple enough to treat in the same sentence? This lady was either crazy or extremely wise. I took my chances and followed her recommendations precisely. I only ate a plant-based, raw diet, juiced a cocktail of plants and vegetables three times a day, and consumed snake oil and three different teas a day. I cleansed with this diet for the duration of my trip and felt so energized. So much so, that I knew I not only needed to visit here but I needed to move here for a year and learn from this gifted soul. I needed to change my life and return to nature.

My stay with Sarah ended much too soon. There was so much more I needed to learn here. I had to leave but I was certain I would be back. As soon as I got home to my family, I made it clear, I was moving to Costa Rica for a year. I started telling everyone this. My family, friends, coworkers, my family doctor, even Aida. I was manifesting, acting like it was already a done deal. Wayne Dyer teachers about using "I am" messages rather than "I will". This way of speaking made sense to me, thus I applied it. "I am living in Costa Rica." Even if I was convinced it was what I needed to do, that Costa Rica was where healing was happening for me, I still had no concrete plan of how this would transpire. I had faith that it would happen. I am doing this! Funny enough, in writing this book, I asked my husband if he recalled the conversation about me moving for a year to Costa Rica. He replied with a puzzled look on his face, "What conversation? It wasn't a conversation, it was more like a monologue on your part," he said. "The girls and I listened to you and we nodded to everything you said. We knew there was no point in contradicting you." Ouch. Thinking of his reply now makes me a little sad. I had listened to my gut and I was driven, and my family supported me. But this just reiterates the importance of putting ourselves first when we need to heal. I made myself a priority.

Disclaimer alert: please do not think that I am telling you to take snake oil, do a plant cleanse, or even fly to Costa Rica. That was *my* journey. What I would like you to take from this is that you should listen to your intuition and let it guide you even if it does not make sense at that moment. As world-famous motivational speaker Tony Robbins would say, "Take action!".[4]

Do something today that you would not have done yesterday. If I was able to step out of my comfort zone and follow my gut, anyone can. I am just the same as you, no better no worse.

"No act of kindness no matter how small
is ever wasted."

-Aesop

CHAPTER 4

MY LIVING FUNERAL AND STARFISH TRIBE

The week of my return home to Canada, something—nothing short of a miracle—happened: The Starfish Tattoo Fundraising Day or, what I call, My Living Funeral. To understand how this event came to be, I need to share a story with you first.

It all started with my daughter Alys telling me I should get a starfish tattoo to cover some bad ink I got when I was 20 years old. She asked (after numerous times of listening to me complain), "Why don't you just get a starfish tattoo to cover it up? They are your favourite and it would mean something.

"You are always telling Lily and me to be kind to others." I thought this was a brilliant idea. You see, I have had a mantra or more like a story I live by. It is called, "The Starfish Story" by Loren Eisley. Some of you may have heard of it. For those who haven't, here is my retelling of this beautiful and heart-warming tale.

One day, an old man was walking along the beach. He saw a figure in the distance that seemed to be dancing. As he strolled closer, he saw that it was a young girl who was running back and forth, throwing starfish back into the ocean as they washed ashore. The old man chuckled and questioned the little one. "Excuse me, but what are you doing there?" "Oh, it is low tide and the starfish are washed up on the sand, so I am putting them back into the sea," she replied. "Well, that's a silly idea. Don't you see there are miles of beaches and hundreds of starfish? It won't make a difference." The child then picked up a starfish and threw it back into the ocean, looked up at the old man and responded with a smile, "It made a difference to that one." Thus, the reason behind getting a starfish tattoo.

As a mom, an educator, and an empath, I spent my life helping others, without giving up on anyone, regardless of their situation. Call me stubborn! Kindness matters. It matters to me. Turns out it mattered to a lot more people than I thought.

Marie was a student of mine, many years ago. She was a happy child filled with light and an exceptional artistic gift. She grew up to be a talented tattoo artist. She designed and tattooed a beautifully detailed starfish on my shoulder blade. When I told her the reason why I wanted this tattoo, she said she also wanted a starfish tattoo. It was a story that she also felt personally connected to. It wasn't until a girlfriend, Isabelle, got a little starfish travelling the globe inked on her foot in my honour, that the starfish event came to be. Isabelle and I were chatting about my quest to find a way to heal, as Marie was working her magic, tattooing her foot. Marie mentioned how much she felt she wanted to give back to me as I had been there for her when she was little. She said that many people want to help me with my mission to find a cure in Costa Rica but didn't know how to help. "Why not make a Starfish Tattoo Event?" she asked. "People can come and get a starfish tattoo in your honour and donate money to help you." I felt skeptical that anyone would want to get a tattoo just like that, humbled by her intention, and very thankful because I really needed financial help.

I was in awe that someone would even think of organizing an event in my honour. I recall sharing the idea a few days later with my friend and colleague, Veronik, who also happened to be a former student of mine. I shared my fear that no one would get tattooed just for me. I said, "That sh*t is permanent!" to which she replied, "Well that's the impact you had on us!"

46

For the first time, as far as I could remember, I surrendered. I let go of all fears and I let myself be helped, even nurtured by my former students, family, friends, and my sea stars.

The day of the Starfish event, dozens of people lined up around the corner to get their tattoos! A total of 57 people were tattooed that day by Marie and two coworkers who generously worked free of charge, giving all their earnings to me. The event was so popular, that a waiting list was created. More than 100 people have been tattooed since. Crazy, right? That day, many came just to see me, hug me, chat with me, or donate money. I had a friend that made starfish cake pops and treats to sell to collect extra money on my behalf. It was estimated that more than 300 people walked into the tattoo parlour that day. They came to show support, compassion, and have a final living moment with me, or so they thought. I realized that family, students, parents, friends, ex-boyfriends, community members, and even strangers lined up to say their goodbyes to me.

It was like they were all paying a last tribute to me, to my memory, but I was still very much alive. What I witnessed that day was my living funeral. It was a day filled with memories and love, tears and laughter. It was MY day. I had never felt so loved, so cared for, so appreciated. My heart overflowed with gratitude. Why do we wait until loved ones are sick or worst, dead, to show or tell them how much they matter and how much we love them? We need to share our hearts and express our love for each other now and every day that follows. It's hard for me to write about this day without getting emotional. My Starfish Tribe was born that day. I think of them often and know that in my journey thriving with cancer, they are with me. We never know the impact of our smiles, hugs, and gestures can have on others. Trust me, humans are amazing. When you need them, they step up. Don't be afraid to ask for help. We should be able to receive a little of what we put out there. We are never alone. You are not alone. I am already part of your tribe.

"To become a butterfly, you must want to fly so much that you are willing to give up being a caterpillar."

-Winnie the Pooh

CHAPTER 5

DOING WHATEVER IT TAKES!

Following The Starfish Event, my sister-in-law, along with my dear friends Shannon and Nik, started a GoFundMe fundraiser to further help earn funds to make my move to Costa Rica a possibility. It was very successful and provided me with enough money to make my desire a reality. Now, there were no obstacles in the way. The coast was clear. I had the money to do this. Sure, I would not live an affluent, rich life, but I would be fine. One last important detail, my family. Were they ready to let me go? Were they going to be ok? Oddly enough, we never sat down to discuss me moving away for a year. My husband and daughters to this day tell me that I was so convinced I was going, that they dared not stand in my way. They accepted the situation (not without pain and a little resentment, I learned later). Regardless, they supported me. They sacrificed having a mom and living without a spouse, putting my needs before theirs. Back then, I was solely focused on my mission to find a cure. I did not realize just how selfless my daughters and husband had to be to make it all happen. I am so blessed to call them my family. I can never thank them enough for believing in me and loving me enough to let me go.

For this separation to happen as smoothly as possible, we decided to vacation to Costa Rica as a family for a couple of weeks first. Then my girls and husband, Sylvain, would fly back to Canada leaving me to start my journey.

We spent two weeks walking in the jungle, swimming in waterfalls, body surfing in the ocean, and laughing, making the best of our time together. The last day of our trip came too rapidly. We decided to spend it on Marino Ballena, our favourite beach in Uvita. While Sylvain and Lily-Rose were running ahead to catch some green waves, Alys and I walked behind both, enjoying what we knew were to be our last moments together for a while. We stopped as our feet touched the ocean and watched our two surfers patiently waiting for the perfect wave. I could not help but feel guilt and sadness. After all, I was the one who was leaving them.

At that very moment, something magical happened. A little girl, who was no more than five years old, tapped me on the side of my left thigh. I turned to face her. She was a beautiful child with long black hair wearing nothing but a bright pink bathing suit. She spoke up, "Mira! Mira!" I looked down and noticed she was holding a bright orange starfish in her hand. My jaw dropped and I replied, "Wow, que linda!" That means 'how cute' and just about as much Spanish I could speak at the time. She started rambling on. I know she was talking about the sea star because I understood the words: "Estrella del mar" but that was it. I simply smiled and looked at Alys who was also in awe over this little girl and her starfish. From afar, her father called her name. He must have asked her to join him because she squatted down, reached out her hand as far as she could into the ocean and released the starfish back to its natural habitat. She smiled, waved, and ran toward her father. Alys grabbed my hand and looked at me with her mouth wide open. "What just happened?" she asked. I was frozen there with my two feet in the sand in disbelief. *Why did this little girl come to me?* She could not have known what a starfish meant to me. Why did she so lovingly let it go right in front of me, on the very last day I was spending with my family? Yes, it was yet another sign. I call this sign, "Slap in the face in case you were wondering, duh! You are exactly where you should be." I knew that here, in this beautiful country, I would grow my starfish tribe and continue to make a difference. I would be supported and safe. Alys and I hugged both still humbled by what just occurred. We let go of our embrace and hurried to tell our family about the wonderful moment that little innocent child shared with us.

The beautiful day came to an end. It was time to say our goodbyes. I recall driving to Dominical, a nearby city, to meet up with the man who would give my family a ride to the airport. The drive was 20 minutes long, but it flew by. We blasted Bob Marley's music with the windows rolled down, not wanting to say goodbye. We wanted to enjoy our time as a unit until the very last moment. When we arrived in this little town, the cab was already there waiting. I hugged my husband, squeezed him so hard, and promised him I would be okay. We were both sobbing but managed to say tonnes of I love you's. Next, it was Lily-Rose's turn. I hugged her and felt a distance. She was never good at goodbyes and refused to see me cry. She simply said, "Be safe. I love you." with little emotion in her voice. "I love you, most sunshine…" I answered trying to hold back my tears. She then walked over to the cab leaving me with Alys who was already visibly upset. We shared a hug that required no words. We couldn't speak. She too headed into the car that would take my family away. "I love you so much, my babies. I love you mon amour," I managed to blurt out before breaking down into an uncontrollable sob. Off they went leaving me alone in the middle of the road melting and drowning in my tears. What have I done?

The drive back to my new tropical home seemed to last for hours. I felt nauseated and hollow, like a piece of me was missing. It was a mix of fear, sadness, and guilt. Too late to turn back now. I needed to suck it up but felt so broken. I could not see how I would be able to pull myself together. I got home, sat on the corner of my bed, and stared out into the jungle. I had no tears left to cry. I felt a little better when I received a text from them telling me they were ok now and about to board the plane. Still, I knew it would take some time before I would feel somewhat whole again. This healing business was going to be a lot more difficult than I thought. Still, I was doing this. I was doing this for them too.

A few days passed, where I found myself torn between fully enjoying the warm weather and the sea, and staying home to drown in my sorrow. One night, to distract myself, I put a load of dirty clothes in the washer. I had put off doing laundry or any other house chores because I wanted to spend every minute enjoying my family. I then called my mother. Who better to talk to when you're sad than your mom? We had been talking for a good 10 minutes when I noticed some water on my bedroom floor. I walked closer to the door, opened it and saw that the kitchen and the living room were completely flooded with at least two inches of water everywhere! The washing machine was not properly installed, and water was gushing out of the hose all over the floor. Without hesitation, I was able to stop the machine from continuing its cycle but what was I going to do about the flooded house? If my husband were here, he would know how to clean up this mess. I was emotionally drained, alone, and had no clue where to begin. I tried using every towel and dishrag in the house but that barely soaked up a few drops. I was dealing with a flood here not a spill. Feeling defeated, I sat on the kitchen floor in the middle of the endless puddle, buried my face in my hands and sobbed like a baby. This was it. This was my breaking point. I couldn't do this...I breathed deeply and closed my eyes. Oddly enough, something inside me said, "Girl, fix your ponytail and get up!" I obeyed. I realized that no one was going to save me. I had to help myself, much like my quest to heal my cancer. I picked up a dustpan and a water cooler. I proceeded to scoop up water with the dustpan and dump it in the cooler until it was full. Then dragged it to the back door and dumped it outside. I must have done this sequence for three hours straight all while asking myself, *If you think this is too much, how are you going to heal cancer then?* I continued until every drop was gone. What happened to me that night is what I think they call: The Dark Night of the Soul. It is the lowest of lows, the bottom of the barrel. That moment could have broken me, led me to throw in the towel (literally, for that matter), and hop on a plane back home, to my safety net. Instead, it made me rise to the occasion and pushed me to do something I thought I could never do alone. Willpower is key on your journey to a better, healthier you. You are the only one standing in your way.

"Let thy food be thy medicine and medicine be thy food."

-Hippocrates

CHAPTER 6

DO YOU WANT TO LIVE?

In 1998, at 22 years old, I was diagnosed with Rheumatoid Arthritis. I was on heavy medications and exhausted all the time. I felt as though I was a porcelain doll that could break if someone touched me. The kind gesture of someone holding out their hand for me to shake made me quiver. A handshake meant pain, opening the fridge door meant pain, going up the stairs meant pain. I even needed my husband's help to get dressed. At that time, I also consulted a naturopath to see if I could do anything to help. He told me I was intolerant to gluten. Back in the 1990s, gluten was a foreign word to me and most of western civilization. The only store that had any gluten-free products was a 45-minute drive from my house. If the distance wasn't enough to discourage me from making the switch to a gluten-free diet, then the taste would do it. The bread tasted like cardboard and pasta like baking soda. To make matters worse, the cost of these not so tasty items were expensive. Needless to say, it was difficult for me to maintain this diet. Nonetheless, being intolerant to gluten was always at the back of my head.

Fast forward 16 years to the first cancer diagnosis, after 33 radiation treatments to "fix" my first cancer I thought, well let me try this gluten-free diet once more. I no longer wanted strong medication in my body. I felt as though I was so radioactive that I would activate metal detectors! I needed to give my body a break from the medication and treatments. I had a gut feeling that gluten was responsible for the inflammation in my body. Consuming foods that you are intolerant to is probably not good for you. After what I had just been through, I no longer wanted to suffer. I was pleasantly surprised to see that in 2014 every grocery store had gluten-free (GF) products. Most of the GF foods I tried were tasty and a lot more affordable. This time I could make the change.

The results of this diet on my body were phenomenal. I no longer showed symptoms of rheumatoid arthritis! I could not only do all the simple daily tasks without pain, but I could do things I had not done in years such as cartwheels and squats. I've been gluten-free since February 27, 2014 and have no arthritic pain. How incredible is that? I had found the recipe that worked for me! I was convinced that food was medicine. Now, what did this mean for my cancer? What kinds of foods would help nurture my body to health? I was curious...

Before moving to Costa Rica, I followed a strict Ketogenic diet. This way of eating involves eating a whole lot of fats. I was never a meat eater so the foods I ate became redundant. I never looked forward to meals and had lost a lot of weight and my appetite. It all felt unnatural. I kept feeling I needed vitamin C. Deep down, I knew that I was going to kick this diet to the curb when I got to Costa Rica. I knew that fresh fruits and vegetables were abundant there. It seemed like a logical, healthy, and cost-efficient choice. I read that a plant-based diet proved to be effective in healing many cancers. One person who had adopted a plant-based diet was named Chris Wark. I stumbled upon one of his YouTube videos while researching plant-based diets. One of the videos that caught my eye was called, "SQUARE ONE Module 1- First Things First".5 I watched that video with complete admiration for this brave man. I felt he was speaking directly to me. I trusted him instantly. I went ahead and invested in the full Square 1 package. I needed guidance to leap fully into a plant-based diet, and who better than Chris to do it, a man who healed stage three cancer himself.

He was a no-bullshit kind of guy. He shared my opinion about cancer: that we created our cancer and that this, in turn, meant we could also heal it. He was speaking my language. He started the video by asking his viewers, *why do you think you have cancer?* I had already done lots of thinking on the issue, so I was comfortable answering. Then, he asked, *do you want to live?* This question shocked me. Of course, I wanted to live! Do you think I would be here alone in Costa Rica right now if I didn't? Don't all cancer patients want to live? It was wrong for me to assume. We must never judge others who are dealing with the disease. Many think that cancer is simply too much and too scary to face. Cancer has such a negative stigma attached to it. When we hear the word *cancer* most of us hear death. So why bother trying, when we are destined to die anyway? In writing this book, I humbly hope that my story will change the way you view cancer. When you think about it, as cancer thriver and influencer, Nalie Agustin says, "Life is a terminal condition." No one is getting out alive. So why are we so shocked when cancer gives a call to remind us that we are not immortal?

Back to Chris Wark and his question: *Do you want to live?* He continued to say that healing cancer was a full-time job, total commitment, no excuses. He went on by saying that if we were not fully invested then this program was not for you. He explained that cancer patients who heal have two characteristics in common: 1) They have a strong will to live; and, 2) They are willing to do whatever it takes to get well. They must be willing to change everything. I thought *that's me.* I am here miles from home willing to do whatever it takes to heal. He was telling me to listen to my instincts and research my disease. I finished watching this video feeling excited, empowered, and convinced that Chris was someone I needed to listen to. I became a devoted student.

The radical change from Ketogenic to a plant-based diet was the first big step I took for my health in Costa Rica. It was so easy for me to buy fresh organic fruits and vegetables here. I always joke and say that the first time I ate a banana I had an orgasm (remember now, I hadn't had a banana in over a year, no judgement please)! I ate three plant-based meals a day, mostly raw, and supplemented with lots of medicinal plants that Aida so carefully prepared for me. Every Sunday I would drive to her minimalist home with the breathtaking view. She would walk me through her garden collecting my "medicine" for the week, taking the time to explain the benefits of each plant. Plants are nature's way to heal. At first, I did not understand a word she was saying, and she couldn't comprehend me either. It didn't matter to us however, every Sunday was spent together collecting plants and cooking. Aida made it her mission to teach me how to prepare and cook food. She collected fruits, vegetables, flowers and herbs, and shared with me how to make savoury raw and cooked dishes. "Voy enseignar como cuisinar," she would teach me how to cook. And did she ever! I learned how to make the best coconut ceviche and green papaya picadillo.

After we cooked together, we always shared a meal. One time, our meal even included a snake! I remember her telling me that I was going to eat snake that day but that she had made my plate so beautiful that I would enjoy it. She was right, it was lovely. Garnished with flowers and heart-shaped vegetables. She told me that if I looked at the food and thought it was nice and healing, then it would be beneficial and healing for my body. This idea of welcoming and thanking food for helping me with my healing process is something I still do today. She went on to explain that a snake could regenerate. With every ounce of snake oil I drank, it was as if was introducing a new healthy cell in my body. If you have one healthy cell that means you are not dead, she explained. Eating a mostly raw plant-based diet has the same benefits; it just takes longer. Who was I to contradict her great wisdom? Even though we had a language barrier, it did not stop us from connecting. Thank God for Google Translate for helping with our communication hurdles. My Spanish improved as our friendship grew. I seriously felt as though she became my second mom. She would remind me that I was family now and that I was strong, "Mui forte". She would proudly giggle and say I was "gorda" (chubby) now. Gaining a little weight meant that I was doing better emotionally and physically.

Chris and Aida were two great masters on my path to better health. They both provided great tips and tricks but the work had to be done by me and me alone.

I not only needed to change my diet but also my mindset and my lifestyle. There is no magic pill when it comes to healing cancer. As Chris explained so well, it takes total commitment. Changing the foods I put in my mouth was my first step. I was faced with temptation almost daily, whenever I drove by the bakery, ate with friends, ordered at the restaurant, or had late-night cravings. I questioned my choices. However, I started to ask, *do I want to feed my body … or feed my cancer?*

"Every time you eat or drink, you are either feeding disease or fighting it."

-Heather Morgan MS, NLC

When you become conscious of what you are putting in your mouth, of what it will do inside your body, you can't help but ask yourself, *do I really want that?* After all, you are what you eat.

"You don't have to have it all figured out to move forward...just take the next step."

-Anonymous

CHAPTER 7

BUILDING MY THRIVER MORNING ROUTINE

In this chapter, I will go into detail about my daily routine. It is a routine I developed with time through research, trial and error, and listening to my body. I am sharing this with you to inspire you, to create a routine that makes sense for you. I am by no means saying to follow all I have done. Rather, what I am trying to say is, *seek your own way.*

I used to think people who were disciplined and needed to do things in a certain way were trapped and stuck in a relentless, boring routine. However, I now understand that through discipline comes freedom. A few weeks ago, I happened to watch the Social, a daytime talk show, while folding a load of laundry when a young man named James Clear was interviewed. He was presenting his book called Tiny Changes, Remarkable Results Atomic Habits[6]. It piqued my curiosity, so I listened to what he had to say. "Boring is freedom!" He explained that people who have the worst exercise habits are the most tired. People who have the worst financial habits are always worried about money. They are the ones that are not free. "Habits do not restrict freedom, they create it!" James Clear understood the importance of a sustainable routine. Let me continue and explain my own.

Living a new life in this strange country, I was faced with having to relearn a new routine. Nothing here was the same as in Canada.

The food, the environment, and the overall mindset were a complete contrast to North American ways. Every morning, I started my day with the one thing I was able to bring back from my hometown, yoga. I started practicing yoga shortly after the recurrence diagnosis. I attended a hot yoga studio twice a week and would practice on my own every morning. Yoga was the one thing I knew for sure was working for me. Every time I stepped onto my mat, I felt connected to my inner voice. I felt a sense of growing peace and harmony. I was taking the time to listen to my breath. I felt alive. I knew that yoga was going to remain an essential tool in my healing journey. After a few chaturanga and warrior poses, I felt energized. I ended each practice sitting in "easy pose" with both hands together in prayer, breathing. I would recite my mantra: *With every breath, I am healed. I have a vividly healthy body.* I would state this as though it had already happened. I learned through research on the power of the mind, that our brain does not distinguish between what is real and what is imagined. I decided to use this to my advantage: *With every breath,*

I am healed. I have a vividly healthy body, I repeated this as often as I could. We breathe quite a bit in a day thus providing us with equal opportunities to heal as well.

Following this peaceful morning practice, I would get up and proceed to do a series of jumping jacks. I had read that the lymphatic system was an important part of our immune system. I also knew that cancer patients have a weakened immune system. Due to my first bout with cancer, I had to get my salivary gland removed. I knew that I had a break in my lymphatic system where the salivary gland had been and needed to do something about it. Both Ty Bollinger (The Truth About Cancer) and Tony Robbins (Motivational speaker and life coach) raved about the benefits of using a rebounder (a mini trampoline) to activate their lymphatic system. I did not have access to such sophisticated equipment in this third world country, but I made do. Jumping jacks gave me a good energy boost every morning.

The next step to my morning routine involved me enjoying a cup of green tea in the sun. Green tea is naturally alkaline. I wanted to start my day off by creating an alkaline environment in my gut. Cancer can only prosper in an acidic terrain. So yes, I gave up coffee and chose to feed my body and not my cancer day in and day out. While browsing on the internet, I discovered Dr. Sebi who was a well-known herbalist who preached about the healing power of an alkaline diet. He was far from being the only doctor I heard profess the benefits of an alkaline body.

I drank this warm cup of tea outdoors, no matter what. I chose my seat so I could face the sun and absorb as much yummy sunlight and natural vitamin D as possible. On my quest to find out all I could about cancer, I learned that we should always start our day outdoors. This allows the sun to send a message to our brains that it is daytime, time to get up and do your thing. It is a way to be in sync with our innate cycle.

My morning routine would not be complete without breakfast. As you already know from reading the last chapter, I had chosen to eat a plant-based organic diet. Kriss Carr, best-selling author, health advocate, and cancer thriver explained that "There's a great metaphor that one of my doctors uses: If a fish is swimming in a dirty tank and it gets sick, do you take it to the vet and amputate the fin? No, you clean the water. So, I cleaned up my system. By eating organic raw greens, nuts and healthy fats, I am flooding my body with enzymes, vitamins, and oxygen." I share Carr's view about cleaning our system. I ate mostly raw fruits and vegetables that were in season. I did not buy any prepackaged foods and stayed away from sugar. My breakfasts consisted mostly of a smoothie made up of fruits, seeds, greens (such as kale) and medicinal plants carefully chosen by Aida. I chose only to savour this first meal at 10 am. I did so to respect my natural biological clock. I practiced intermittent fasting which meant that I ate all my meals between 10 am and 6 pm. Here is why I did it: According to John Douillard DC.[7] Ayurveda medicine video available on Gaia, our body has two 12-hour cycles in a day. The first one starts at sunrise from 6 to 10 am. It's the optimal time to exercise as our bodies are the strongest during this time frame. Between 10 am and 2 pm, it is the time when our digestive system is at its best. It is during this time frame that we should eat most of our calories. Our biggest meal should be lunch. We must eat a hearty lunch to keep us from having those afternoon cravings. Between 2 and 6 pm is the time our nervous system is the most active and will crave sugar. The second cycle starts at 6 pm and lasts until 10 pm. It's during this time that we should slow down, prepare our body to relax, and settle down for bed. Between 10 pm and 2 am, the body detoxifies, repairs, and heals, that is if you don't eat or get up and watch TV. The only way your body can heal is if you respect its natural cycle. If you snack between these hours, you are stopping your body from doing what it naturally needs to do. It will stop the detoxification process and will go back to digestion. The same goes for sleep. If you stay up later than 10 pm you are preventing your body from starting its regenerating job. When you have cancer or any disease for that matter, is it not better to work with our bodies than against it? Finally, between 2 and 6 am, the nervous system activates once again, getting us ready to rise and shine. If you would like to learn more about the basics of Ayurveda, I recommend researching the works of John Douillard DC.

What I have been describing thus far, as my morning routine, may seem overwhelming and maybe even impossible for you to attain. Rest assured, it was not always easy for me and still can be a challenge to find the motivation and time to respect this process. James Clear, whom I mentioned earlier, spoke about rearranging your home to make things conducive to change. For example, why not reposition the armchair to face the coffee table with a stack of books on it, instead of directly at the TV. In my current home in Quebec, my husband built a yoga mat rack and mounted it on the wall right outside my bedroom. It is the first thing I see when I open the door. It's a daily morning reminder that this is my first go-to activity of the day.

In the television interview, Mr. Clear also spoke about taking action, "Every action you take is like a vote for the type of person you want to become. No, meditating for one minute will not make you calm, but it does cast a vote for; I am a meditator." He then advises how to make changes. He shared what he calls the *2-Minute Rule*, "Take whatever habit you are trying to build and scale it down to something that takes two minutes or less to build. So do yoga four times a week, becomes take out my yoga mat... the whole point here's that a habit needs to be established before it can be improved."

I simply could not have explained this better myself. We often are way too critical and judgmental towards ourselves. This 2-Minute Rule is something that makes any desired habit into something doable. If only I had heard James's wise advice before, I would have avoided lots of negative self-talk!

I have attributed my ability to take action, in part to Tony Robbins and his Breakthrough program[8]. Just before I went to Costa Rica, Rachel, another former student of mine and beautiful light in this world, visited me. She was so passionate about the work of Tony Robbins, that I remember listening to her and drinking in her words. She was barely 30 years old and yet was one of the brightest people I knew. She said Tony Robbins would be key in my journey to self-healing and self-growth. She was so convinced that she offered me his Breakthrough program. I was humbled by her generosity and in awe of her motivation. She set up an account for me and wrote my password on a Post-it Note so I could remember it. It read: *I am the shit!* Now, I know we should not share passwords but got to love her sense of humour. I never had any trouble logging in.

For those of you who are not familiar with Tony Robbins, he is a giant man who made it his life's work to empower others to live their best lives. The Breakthrough program is intended for us to reflect upon our behaviours, our emotions, our decisions, our mindset, and much more. It also motivates us with powerful talks by Tony and other individuals who themselves struggled through life. The end goal is to become who you were always meant to be, to live your true purpose. This course was a daily commitment of at least 30 minutes. I would first listen to the talks and then I had some homework to do. Some days the work was easier than others. I remember a section of the course was devoted to relationships. During that particular part, I struggled every day not wanting to face what Tony had in store for me. I wasn't even living with my husband! How could I work on my relationship? I was faced with my insecurities. It forced me to ask real questions and make tough decisions and realizations on all aspects of my life. However, eating breakfast with Tony Robbins hyping me up became a vital part of my daily routine.

This motivational speaker taught me that when you are willing to do the work, anything is possible. "Whatever you want in life, study it," he says. It's never too late to live out your full potential. He was also able to guide me into finding my purpose, which I was able to write down and display on my fridge so I could see it every day: *My purpose is to heal, so I can help guide others to a healthy, cancer-free life.*

I encourage you to set up morning habits that work for you. Do your own research and try things out. To help you get started, here's a summary of what I considered when creating mine:

- Cancer primarily feeds on sugar. Learn to read labels and avoid refined sugars at all costs.

- A healthy mindset is key in knowing we have the power to thrive and even heal cancer. Find a mantra or positive affirmation that empowers you from the moment you get up.

- Reduce your stress levels. Take time to be with yourself. Learn to be silent through yoga, meditation, or simple breathwork.

- Cancer does not like oxygen. An activated healthy lymphatic system will help your immune system grow stronger. Incorporate some morning exercises that stimulate your body and get your blood pumping.

- Choose your breakfast foods wisely. The ideal being foods which are in season, organic, and alkaline. Prioritize fruits and vegetables.

- Respect your body's natural cycle. Try to eat during the ideal period between 10 am to 6 pm.

As Tony Robbins said in one of his later lectures in the Breakthrough Program, "Trust in God but tie your camels!" Your faith may light the way, but you need to also help yourself.

"If you don't make time for your wellness, then you will have to make time for your illness."

-Anonymous

CHAPTER 8

HEALING IS A FULL-TIME JOB!

Costa Rica began to feel more and more familiar. It helped that my daughter Alys decided to drop everything and join me in October. Her presence gave me the strength I needed to do whatever it took to heal. I kept thinking that if I can thrive with cancer, then maybe she would not have to go through this ordeal herself. This gave me further motivation to stick to my new healthy lifestyle.

Our days were mostly quiet and stress-free. We spent a good chunk of our time collecting and preparing food together. We enjoyed inventing new, fresh dishes that tasted delicious. We played around with "ceviche" and "picadillo" recipes, adding whatever veggies we could get our hands on at that moment (see the last chapter for Aida's original recipes). Cooking alongside my daughter every day was such a blessing. If she could learn at 17 the importance of eating healthy, she would flourish into adulthood. After all, if you don't take care of your body, where are you going to live?

Other than food preparation, Alys and I focused on learning and enjoying time spent within our new community. She worked on her online classes and volunteered in a no-kill animal shelter. I facilitated learning at a local school. As for the rest of my time, I would also research, read, watch, and learn all I could about cancer and healing my body.

As soon as 4 pm came, Alys and I would head to the beach for an afternoon walk and our favourite activity, watching the sunset. Watching the sun slowly descend to the sea brought me immense gratitude. I felt thankful for my family, for the chance I had to be here, and yes, I eventually even caught myself being thankful for my cancer. Without it, I would not be on this beach, enjoying a miracle of nature.

Watching the sunset was a time to meditate with my eyes open and to recite my mantra. This practice soothed my worries and calmed my mind. I later learned of something called sun gazing that explained the blissful feeling that was induced by watching the days come to an end. Sungazing is the act of looking directly at the sun during dusk or dawn. According to Dawn James at raisethevibartion.ca[9], the benefits of this practice include activating areas of the brain that are currently dormant, bringing balance to the mind, encouraging a positive mindset, boosting confidence, facilitating the way we solve problems, and much more. At the time, I had no idea why I felt compelled to watch every sunset and stare at the sun. Once I heard about sungazing, it all made sense. I was simply following my intuition and it wasn't misguiding me.

My daily walks on the beach were also vital to me. I needed to stroll barefoot on the sand every day. The feeling induced by the warm sand between my toes was empowering. I was part of something bigger. I felt connected to everything and everyone but especially to nature. I was exactly where I needed to be, strong and fearless. I was curious about that sense of connectivity and power. I read up on the benefits of being in nature. Turns out the benefits are endless! In my research, I learned about "grounding" or "earthing" from the documentary, Heal for Free[10]. The pull to connect with Mother Earth was a common phenomenon. When our body makes direct contact with the earth, it receives a dose of energy that makes us feel better rapidly. It's scientifically proven to have many healing benefits. You can read the article in Healthline. com by Eleesha Lockett, MS entitled, "Grounding: Exploring Earthing Science and the Benefits Behind It" to find out more.

I simply cannot stress how important it is to go outdoors, to spend time in nature, and take off our shoes. Direct contact is the key to obtaining the full benefits of Mother Nature's love!

After our time on the beach, the evenings were spent preparing fresh, organic dinners. Good food takes time! I did not want to negate my hard work by throwing together a last-minute meal. Thus, the creativity and participation of my daughter were significant. After preparing our "ceviche" or "picadillo" of the day, we sat down together at the table and shared conversation. It was a time we often took to video call our two other beloved family members back home in Canada. Speaking to my husband and daughter Lily-Rose was essential. I needed to know everything I had missed that day. They kept me updated on all that was going on in their lives, sometimes even complaining about each other. I listened but knew very well there was not much I could do about it. Technology was a blessing during our time apart. I benefited from their love and support even if they were miles away. I missed them dearly. Sometimes seeing them would fill me up with so much joy and other days I would hang up feeling a massive void within me. This was only temporary, I kept reminding myself. I knew we would be reunited at Christmas.

Every night since my arrival in Costa Rica, I would make it a point to go to bed early. I wanted to give my body all the time it needed to repair and restore. More often than not, I was fast asleep by 9:30 pm. Most nights I listened to guided meditations in my bed. If I lied down, I would fall asleep before the end, so I sat up and breathed in and out slowly, calming my mind, letting my thoughts be guided by the voice of a stranger whose sole purpose at the time, was to help me unwind.

If you have never meditated or think you can't do it, I recommend you try and not be too hard on yourself. It takes practice to quiet the mind. I still have days where my mind is uncooperative and simply will not settle. It is just one thought after another. I persist anyway, continuously bringing my awareness back to my breath. Some days I succeed with ease and achieve a state of serenity. Other days, I am only able to focus on my breathing for seconds at a time without being carried away by my thoughts. We need to accept this and be kind to ourselves. With practice, meditation does get easier. If you don't succeed with one type of meditation, try another. You may find a guided meditation that involves visualization easier to start with. However, if this format is not for you, then try a body scan or breathwork. Just keep searching until you find what is just right for you. When you do, it is amazing what you can hear in the silence.

My daily habits were influenced by the book, "How to Make Disease Disappear" by Dr. Rangan Chatterjee[11]. This doctor speaks about a form of medicine that starts in your home. "You don't have to die; you don't even have to be sick. You just need to change your lifestyle." Dr. Chatterjee is changing the way patients and practitioners view health. He shares with his readers the 4 pillars to a healthy body and mind: Relax, Eat, Sleep, and Move. Each section explains the importance of a specific pillar and goes on to offer examples of how you can incorporate this in your daily life. I highly recommend this book to help you build your healthy habits.

I have shared with you what works for me, however, learning what works best for you matters most. Remembering that all it takes to start is a step in the right direction. You do not have to change everything at once.

As yoga osteopath Patrick Salibi[12] author of the book "L'Experience Humaine", once said in a conference I attended, "You simply need to start to take Response-Ability for your health." We need to stop solely looking to everyone and everything else for answers. We must learn to trust our inner voice and feel what is right for us. During one of his conferences, Salibi spoke about the human loss of intuition. People turn to Google to make sense of their aches and pains. Rarely do they stop and take the time to reflect on what they might be doing to cause their illness. I invite you to reconnect with yourself, be still, and listen to what your body is trying to tell you. Remember, don't be too hard on yourself. Just take one small step towards creating a healthier, happier you.

"Everything you need your courage, strength, compassion and love: everything you need is already within you."
-Anonymous

CHAPTER 9

BACK TO REALITY

After the holidays spent in my hometown of St-Jean-sur-Richelieu, Canada, my husband and youngest daughter Lily-Rose came to live with Alys and me in our little tropical paradise. It was soothing and motivating to have them with me. My husband realized just how stressed he was and started to make lasting changes. He became a runner and he enjoyed my plant-based meals. For Lily-Rose, it was a different story. She never did well with change. Though she showed great compassion toward me, she was unhappy in Costa Rica. Being away from her friends and homeschooling turned out to be too much for her to handle. After many difficult talks and some disagreements, the four of us came to a united decision. It would be best if Lily-Rose and Sylvain returned to Canada. We needed to put her needs and education first. The time apart wouldn't be as long this time. We did it once, we could do it again.

They took a plane back to Montreal in April of 2019 and left Alys and me behind. The separation was trying, to say the least. Watching the cab drive away with half of my precious family opened a sensitive wound. I consoled myself, hugging Alys. I was grateful that I was able to spend four months as a family unit. It was comforting to realize that during their time in this foreign country, they both gained a clear understanding of why I was doing this and were convinced I would be okay. Heck, I would flourish! It wasn't until my daughter Alys left in May that I was faced with truly being alone. I began to wonder why I was still here.

I still had two months before my return date. *What else did I have to learn?* The answer, I soon found out, pertained to my spiritual growth. I had worked for months on my body and mind but had neglected my soul.

An awesome perk of Costa Rica that may not be well-known, is that many holistic practitioners come to escape the fast pace life found in Western countries. These professionals are content with the stress-free lifestyle even if it could mean earning less money. Appointments and events organized by these practitioners were abundant. It was my soul sister and friend Kristin, whom I met in Uvita shortly after I arrived, that said to me "Girl, we are still here for a couple of months. Let's make the most out of it!" That, we did. We went to yoga therapy classes, breathwork sessions, and bio-resonance appointments. One evening, we went to a sound bowl healing event. It was an intimate venue that allowed for an immediate sense of connectedness, both to the singing bowls and Dawn James, the leader of the session. She shared her life story and said something that strongly resonated with me. She explained that the body we live in is simply loaned to us. When talking about our physical, she went on to say that it is simply the bodysuit that we live in. It has an unknown expiry date on it yet we don't know when we must return it. It is what is inside that bodysuit that lives on.

That analogy helped me put things in perspective and validated my need for spiritual growth. I loved the experience. I felt as though I was flying, lifted by the powerful vibrations produced by crystal bowls. I needed Dawn's help to fully ground myself back to my yoga mat afterwards, as I still felt like I was floating. (If you can't relate to this feeling, the closest thing I can compare it to is trying to focus on a serious conversation while having one too many glasses of wine.) On our way out, Kristin insisted that I tell Dawn about my cancer journey. I was a bit reluctant, so she spoke up. She shared that I had a cancer recurrence and that I travelled here on a mission to get well. Mrs. James smiled and said, "I would be really curious to hear your full story." We planned to meet for lunch later that week at a local restaurant we both loved. I instantly felt comfortable in her presence. I shared my story, trying not to leave out too many details. She also shared some of hers. I remember her looking me in the eyes and saying, "I think you're ready." *Ready for what?* I thought. It was then that Dawn made me realize that I had a book in me. I was ready to share my story. I never thought of writing a book and certainly never considered myself an author. She was so convincing, I knew I had to write this book. My date with Dawn was the last meaningful encounter I had in Costa Rica.

Two days later, I was on a flight heading back home to Montreal, Quebec. On the plane, I was lucky enough to be bumped up to business class. I had lots of legroom and special treats. I took this as yet another sign that the universe had my back. I pulled out Dawn James's book, "How to Raise the Vibrations Around You"[13]. A gift she had generously offered all for attending the singing bowl evening. This book included tons of helpful tips on how to make your home a healthy, pollution-free place to live. I carefully took down notes on how to improve the air and water quality of my home. I wrote down the names of plants that were natural air purifiers and created a list of the best essential oils to diffuse. I knew I wanted my house to be the best, purest, and most healing home someone could live in. I had just spent a year out in the jungle, connected to nature, reaping the benefits of Pura Vida (pure life). There was no way I was going back to my old habits or living in a damaging environment.

By the time my plane landed at Pierre Elliott Trudeau International Airport, I had a plan. I knew what to do to keep my body, mind, and spirit in the best condition possible. I was armed with the knowledge to make my environment—both inner and outer—the perfect place for me to thrive. It was great to walk off the plane feeling so empowered.

My husband, uncle Yves, mom, and dad were all waiting for me. My husband saw me first, he ran up to me and hugged me. Next, my uncle gave me a heartfelt squeeze, followed by my loving parents who embraced me with tenderness. I was home. Seeing them filled me with gratitude. I could have never done it without the support of my loved ones. Thank you, life!

An hour later, Sylvain drove us to our new house. It felt good to be home and to see my daughters. How I missed them. Minutes after my arrival, it felt as though I had never left. That feeling, to my surprise, scared me tremendously. I needed things to be different this time. I wanted to continue to follow my healing routine and to take time for myself daily. Adjustments needed to be made for me to not revert to old habits.

I was and still am very blessed to have two daughters and a husband who are open-minded and love me very much. We had many conversations about boundaries and family harmony. Our nest was a haven for us, a stress-free place where we could be ourselves. My family accepted me and who I had become. I felt they understood me but I know very well that they thought I was a little crazy when I stood and smiled at the sun, hugged trees, enjoyed a green leafy meal, smudged the house with sage, and avoided the use of the microwave at all cost! But they are just happy they have a mom and a wife who is thriving despite a stage 4 incurable cancer diagnosis.

My external environment now seemed to be under control, but what about my inner environment? How would I maintain the calmness I felt inside? Life here is extremely fast-paced. We are exposed to road rage, Black Friday, reality TV, fast-food restaurants, social media, and more. These chaotic distractions cloud our minds and lead us to believe that that is what life's all about. I wanted to keep my life simple, uncluttered, and uncomplicated.

I had a revelation one day when I walked into a Costco shortly after my return from Costa Rica. There were tons of people in the store each with a shopping cart, speeding to be first to make it to the cashiers. I watched with curiosity. *Why the rush?* I felt a deep sense of detachment. I simply could no longer relate. I was baffled. I looked down, took a breath, and listened to what was going on inside me: only peace. I then placed my hand on my heart. "It is folly to think I can find the peace I need around me. The peace I need is within me." For the first time, I understood that this inner peace is truly all that mattered. Where I stood in the world did not make a difference, as long as I was present and self-aware, I was home.

"Magic happens when you don't give up
even though you want to. The universe
always falls in love with a stubborn heart."
-Anonymous

CHAPTER 10

A HERO'S JOURNEY

When I reflect on how depressed I was sitting in my pyjamas staring blankly into space; then feeling connected and at peace strolling on the beaches of Costa Rica, to now feeling invincible upon my return, I can't help but wonder: *what in the world happened to me?* Sure, I have a strong personality. I spent most of my life in a position of control, being a teacher and a mom. Leaving everything behind and changing my whole life, that was totally out of character for me! The only explanation for what happened to me is that I was called to go on what is known as "A hero's journey".

A hero's journey is when you start in your regular protected world, you then receive a call, and an unexpected pull to do something that is completely out of character. People who receive this call often have an inexplicable feeling that something is off, something's not right. Some people will quit their well-paying, yet stressful jobs without having a plan B. As for me, I was called to leave my work and family behind to move to Costa Rica. The challenge is not only to hear that call but to answer it. If we do not pay attention to this nudge to change, it can come at you as hard as a sledgehammer.

A hero's journey is a lot more common than we think. In nearly all movies, we can see the pattern of a hero's journey take place.

Take the Wizard of Oz, for example. Dorothy, the main character, was facing major conflict with her evil neighbour when a storm took her by surprise and swept her away to an unknown reality. The first step of this journey is separation. During this step, you must follow your gut. I remember my Dad did not want to hear about the Costa Rica project at all. He would say "Shhh, just tell me when you are there." He was merely acting upon his innate need to keep me safe. My mother, on the other hand, listened to me and supported me. I know now that was a lot more challenging for her than it seemed at the time.

The next step is called "initiation". This refers to the many challenges and obstacles the hero must face. Dorothy had to help her friend the Lion find his courage, her friend Tinman find his heart, and her friend Scarecrow find his brain. She also had a dream of her own: to go home to her aunt and uncle. I lived my initiation daily, in the moments I could not share with my family, the foods I could no longer eat, the haunting thought of dying alone but also in unique circumstances like the flooding of my home described earlier in this book. I was tested to overcome my fears and live out my full potential.

On our hero journey, we will have signs and guides along the way. I must admit that there always seemed to be a sign that convinced me time after time that I was exactly where I needed to be. I remember one day walking on the beach I so loved yet sobbing uncontrollably. I was scared I had sacrificed my life with my family for no reason. I feared that death was around the corner and that I had done all these changes for no valid reason. Total self-doubt. I decided to breathe and open my heart. I recited my mantra: *With every breath, I am healed*, over and over again. Anything to stop those negative destructive thoughts from coming. When I came home that day, I shared this on my Facebook page:

"I must admit that I was feeling a little down for the past few days. I have been blessed with the visit of so many loved ones in the past month that it was difficult not to feel a void. I even questioned if it was worth it to stay here until July... It now rains daily and the sky is gray. My family and the Starfish tribe are far away. But I went to the beach today and everywhere I looked was a symphony! The monkeys joyously frolicking in the trees reminded me to enjoy each moment. The splendid red macaws engrossed in passionate discourse with each other reminded me how important community is to all. The magical orchestra of green waves slowly crashing reminded me of my husband and friends that love to ride them, and the gray-blue sky reminded me that not everything has to be bright and clear to be perfect. To top it off, it was mango and avocado season. You cannot walk a minute without finding a fresh mango to pick. A free vegan bar!

As I walked to my car, I found the perfect heart-shaped red leaf. Love and healing are still right here for me! Count your blessings they say, but I am running out of fingers."

I was guided towards optimal health. I saw the signs despite my fear and I kept going. I pushed beyond what I thought I could endure. In the documentary, "Finding Joe", Joseph Campbell, the professor who discovered The Hero's Journey pattern by studying mythology and comparative religion said, "Your life is the fruit of your own doing. You only have yourself to blame for it."[14] Had I thrown in the towel that day, given up, I would not be writing this book right now.

A true hero's journey would not be complete without a dragon. I was not armed with a shield or a sword, all I had was my courage and self-love. The dragon I had to slay had always been within me. The dragon was me! I was the one who was holding me back, the one who doubted me. Courage is what enabled me to risk and take an uncommon path and self-love is what allowed me to heal, thrive, and accept my life despite cancer. Dorothy of the Wizard of Oz also had it in her all along. The red shoes she wore were the secret to her returning home. Glinda the good witch told her, "You've always had the power, my dear. You just had to learn it for yourself." Once she was confident, she clicked her heels three times and was transported back to her beloved home.

The last part of the hero's journey, known as "the return home", is the most important, in my opinion. It is the time you are reunited with your loved ones and share the essence of your journey. It is time to inspire others by what you have learned and encountered. In the documentary "Finding Joe", Deepak Chopra explains that, "If you speak to somebody at the level of the mind, then you speak to their mind. If you speak through your heart then you will speak to the heart. But, if you speak through your life and your life is the story, then you will change lives!"

In writing this book, I humbly wanted to inspire you on your own journey, to be your own hero, to create your own story.

The last little bit I feel I need to share with you is my philosophy about being "cured". I know that for many people dealing with cancer, the ultimate goal is to be cured to move on with life and never look back. I thought the same way for years. With time, I have come to see it differently.

It was one of Kriss Carr's talks that showed me a different way of thinking: "Yes, I have cancer and it might not go away, but I can still have a future because life goes on."[15] For the first time, I allowed myself to just be a person with cancer that may never leave my body. I was lucky to be alive and realized that it did not matter whether I was cured or not. I was going to thrive in my life.

Oddly enough, cancer has become a friend. A quiet friend that occasionally speaks up if she feels misunderstood or neglected. She is always with me reminding me to love myself and to take the best care of my mind, body, and soul. If I had the certainty that I was cured, then maybe in a few months I would forget about this quiet friend. I may start slacking off my healthy diet or exercising less. I may forget to connect with Mother Nature and I may even go back to living a stressful life. By wanting to thrive, I am choosing self-care as a way of life, not a means to an end. In a podcast by cancer thrivers and influencers, Stephanie Seban and Nalie Agustin's, they describe a thriver as "anyone living beyond any adversity."[16] That's the way I choose to live my life.

Now **you**, whoever you are, whether you have cancer, know someone who does, or would like to prevent it, **you**, have the power to thrive. When cancer calls, it is a message no one wants to receive. But, have the courage to pick up the phone and discover the limitless power that is in **you**.

I believe in **YOU**. xx

CONNECT WITH VERO LEMAY

Website

Verolemay.com

Facebook

Vero Lemay author

https://www.facebook.com/whencancercallsanswer/

Instagram

LemayVero

https://www.instagram.com/lemayvero/

MENTORS, EXPERTS, AND RECOMMENDED WORKS

"The expert in anything was once a beginner."
-Anonymous

This chapter is dedicated to podcasts, documentaries, programs, and books that have shaped my life and allowed me to embrace cancer. This list solely includes references mentioned in this book; however, there are so many more that have had an impact on me. Stay curious!

END NOTES

1. Bollinger, Ty M. "The Truth About Cancer, A Global Quest. Episode 1" The Truth About Cancer. TTC Publishing, 2014-2020,LLC [https://go2.thetruthaboutcancer.com/agq/episode-1/]

    Bollinger, Ty M. The Truth About Cancer: Everything You Need to Know About Cancer's History, Treatment and Prevention. Carlsbad: Hay House, Inc., 2016

2. Turner, Kelly A., Ph.D. Radical Remissions: Surviving Cancer Against All Odds. New York: HarperCollins, 2015

3. Dyer, Wayne W. Dr. "The Shift". Hay House. May 1, 2009. [https://www.hayhouse.com/the-shift-online-video]

Dyer, Wayne W. Dr. Wishes Fulfilled: Mastering the art of manifesting Carlsbad: Hay House, Inc., 2012

4. Robbins, Tony. Core Decision Number 3; what are you going to do? Empower yourself through action: why focus and meaning must result in motion. Robbins Research International Inc. March 26, 2016. [https://www.tonyrobbins.com/empower-yourself-through-action/]

Robbins, Tony. I Am Not Your Guru. Berlinger, Joe. Netflix. 14 March 14, 2016. [https://core.tonyrobbins.com/documentary/]

5. Wark, Chris. "Module 1: First Things First" Square One Healing Cancer Coaching Program. Chris Beat Cancer. Nov. 26, 2012. [https://www.chrisbeatcancer.com/module]

6. Clear, James. Atomic Habits: An Easy and Proven Way to Build Good Habits and Break Bad Ones. New York: Penguin and Random House, 16 Oct. 2018

7. Douillard, John Dr. Basis of Ayurveda. Gaia. 2018

8. Robbins, Tony. Breakthrough Program. Robbins Research International Inc. [https://www.tonyrobbins.com/breakthrough-app/]

9. James, Dawn. 8 Reasons to Try Sun Gazing. Raise Your Vibration.ca [https://raisethevibration.ca/8-reasons-to-try-sun-gazing/]

10. Kroschel, Steve. Heal for Free. Gaia. Aug. 8, 2014

11. Chatterjee, Rangan.Dr. How to Make Disease Disappear. New York: Harper One, 2018

12. Salibi, Patrick. L'Expérience Humaine: Un Voyage Initiatique Les Mystères du Corps Humain, de la Vie et du Cosmos. Montréal: Editions Gyann, 2015

13. James, Dawn. How to Raise the Vibration around You: Volume I: Working with the 4 Elements to Create Healthy and Harmonious Living Spaces. Brighton: Lotus Moon Press, 2014

14. Salomon, Patrick Takaya. Finding Joe. Amazon Prime, Gaia. Sept. 30, 2011.

15. Carr, Kriss. How Chris Beat Cancer Interview. YouTube [https://www.youtube.com/channel/UCTMXwu4TgF3j9oHiBn_Iaqw]

16. Agustin, Nalie and Seban, Stephanie. What is Thriver? E8 - Thriver Talks Podcast w/ Stephanie & Nalie. Dec. 5, 2019. Facebook [https://www.facebook.com/watch/?v=683658788826875]

APPENDIX

AIDA'S RECIPES

Aida has permitted me to share some of her typical recipes with you. For those of you who may not have the chance to meet this knowledgeable, caring woman, you can feel her love in your kitchen as you prepare her nutritious recipes. The quantities mentioned below are all approximates, as Aida never cooks with measuring cups and spoons.

Guanabana Tea
(aka, Graviola, Soursop, Corossol)

As you know, Guanabana was the first reason I headed to Costa Rica. I am happy to say that you can find the dried leaves in most natural food stores now. Here is a simple way to make this potent tea. This tea is filled with antioxidants, it reduces inflammation, and works as an antimicrobial.

Ingredients:
- 25-30 Guanabana leaves
- Water

Instructions:
- In a large pot, bring 3 litres of water to a boil.
- Add the Guanabana leaves and let simmer for 7-8 minutes.
- Remove from heat, cover, and let the tea steep for a few hours.
- Refrigerate.
- The tea will be good for a few days in the fridge. You can drink it cold or hot. Never heat the tea in the microwave as you will be

killing its healing properties. Use a kettle or a pot instead. You may sip this tea throughout your day. Take a bit at a time. Allow your body time to get used to it. See how you tolerate it. It can cause nausea.

Jugo de Sangre

Blood juice. Don't worry, this juice is not made with blood! Aida calls it that due to its deep reddish-purple colour. She would tell me I should drink this once a day. This juice is great to boost your immune system. It is filled with essential vitamins and minerals.

Ingredients:
- Equal amounts of:
- Approximately 2 handfuls raw spinach
- Approximately 2 handfuls raw green beans
- 2 medium-sized raw carrots
- 1 large raw beet
- 1 medium raw sweet potato

Optional: to preserve the juice even longer than a few days in the fridge, you can add 1-2 cups of pure, organic, unsweetened, blueberry or grape juice.

Instructions:
If you have a juicer:
- Wash and cut up the vegetables into pieces that will easily be processed by your juicer.
- Simply juice all the vegetables and enjoy!
- Store in fridge

If you have a blender:
- Wash and cut up the vegetables into pieces that will easily be processed by your blender.
- Add the spinach to your blender and blend until you have a liquid texture. You may have to use a few tablespoons of water to help liquefy.
- Take a strainer and place it in a bowl.
- Pour the liquid spinach into the strainer and press on it with your hands, repeatedly, until there is no more juice seeping through the strainer.

- Discard the leftover mixture from the strainer.
- Repeat this process from the beginning with each vegetable.
- Store in the fridge.

Enjoy!

Vegetarian/Vegan Ceviche

A Ceviche is a typical Caribbean dish. In Costa Rica, you can order it at almost every restaurant or pick it up along the side of the road, sold by local merchants. It is typically made with raw fish. All Ceviche have one thing in common: they are marinated with lime and lots of it! Here are seven different varieties made in Costa Rica:

Ingredients:
Base ingredients common to all Ceviche:

- 1 big tomato
- 1 mild pepper
- 1 small hot pepper (to taste)
- 1 small onion

- 1 bunch of fresh cilantro
- 6-8 limes

For the main ingredient choose from:
- A- Half a raw butternut squash
- B- A handful of big radishes
- C- 3 cups of fresh palm hearts
- D- 1 big chayote (mirliton squash)
- E- *Green papaya
- F-*Green banana
- G- 3 cups of coconut flesh

*Fruits like papaya and banana are considered vegetables when they are not ripe. Used commonly in many typical dishes.

Instructions:
- Chop the base ingredients; tomatoes, an onion, peppers, and cilantro into very small pieces.
- Squeeze the limes to extract the juice.
- Mix vegetables and lime juice in a big bowl.
- Select one of the main ingredients (A-G).
- Remove peel and seeds if necessary, and chop into small pieces.

- Add to the lime mixture.
- Let sit for 30 minutes.
- Taste and add more lime if necessary

Note: Most ceviches include some sugar to neutralize some of the bitterness; however, Aida never added any to mine because cancer feeds on sugar.

Green Papaya Picadillo

Picadillo is one of my favourite Costa Rican, warm dish. It is typically made with green papaya or yellow squash depending on what is in season. Aida normally makes this in huge quantities over an outdoor wood burning stove.

Ingredients:

- 1 green papaya or 1 yellow squash (not spaghetti squash)
- Coconut oil about ¼ cup
- 1 onion
- 1 green or red mild pepper
- 4 cloves of garlic

- A bunch of fresh cilantro
- A pinch of salt

Instructions:

(A little advice for this recipe: the smaller you cut the vegetables, the better it tastes!)

- Chop up the onion and the garlic.
- Peel the papaya (or squash) and remove its seeds.
- Chop the peppers in small pieces.
- Chop the cilantro, reserve for the end.
- Add some of the coconut oil to a pan.
- Cook the onion and garlic for a few minutes.
- Add the chopped papaya (or squash)
- Add a pinch of salt.
- Stir constantly. Cook for about 8 minutes.
- Add peppers
- Stir continuously and cook some more. You may need to add more coconut oil to avoid the mixture from sticking.
- Taste the mixture occasionally. It is ready when the papaya (or squash) becomes soft.
- Add cilantro and mix for an extra minute.
- Serve and savour!

Made in the USA
Coppell, TX
10 September 2020

37039700R00085